AUTHOR	CLASS
	LE02

TITLE

MEMORIES OF BLACKPOOL

Foreword

Memories of Blackpool is a compilation of pictures from the not-too-distant past. Each has been selected according to its ability to rekindle memories of days gone by, prompting thoughts of daily life and enjoyable holidays in the *Blackpool* we knew when we were a little younger. From the early days, when workers from the mill towns of Lancashire would descend in droves on the town to enjoy their annual ration of fresh air and relaxation, Blackpool has grown to become everyone's favourite. All manner and means of entertainment followed, each designed to find new ways of providing even more laughter and enjoyment - guaranteeing that the crowds would return year after year in the process. And they did. This modest book is not intended to be a work of local history; it has far more to do with entertainment than serious study, though we have included some dates and statistics where we thought they may prove to be of interest to the reader.

We have been fortunate to have been granted access to some very interesting photographs which chart much of the growth and development of the town. Many theatres, piers and places of entertainment get a mention, as you would expect, and the effect of the railway and tramway system are described here too. Shopping is an important part of our daily lives and this has not been neglected. Many of the larger stores are included and some are seen in the process of building or redevelopment.

Blackpool 'behind the scenes' is represented on the following pages in the form of detailed accounts of the history behind some of the town's most successful business and leisure organisations. We have been fortunate in being allowed access to their private archive material, and interesting reading it makes too! Crowded beaches are a feature of every book about Blackpool, and this one is no exception; scenes in which there barely seems to be a square inch of unoccupied sand highlight the immense popularity that has been associated with Britain's favourite resort. Blackpool Tower is an icon that has been closely linked with the resort since it was constructed over 100 years ago. It was a major feat of engineering at the time and is no less impressive (though rather more taken for granted) to the modern eye. If there was a list of the seven wonders of the *holiday* world Blackpool Tower would certainly be near the top of it!

This brief introduction serves, we hope, to illustrate the breadth of topics covered in the book and to give an impression of the objectives we had when we set out to compile it. Working on Memories of Blackpool has been a pleasure; we hope you enjoy reading it.

Happy memories!

Phil Holland & Mark Smith, Publishers

Unmistakably Blackpool. Like some mass evacuation, every square foot of the beach is accounted for in this view from almost 50 years ago. It was obviously a chilly day judging by the way virtually everyone is wrapped up in coats, hats and headscarves. Most of the holiday makers are either sleeping or dozing in their deckchairs, possibly not the most exciting pursuit in Blackpool, but definitely one of the cheapest!

First published in 1997 by:
True North Books
Dean Clough
Halifax
HX3 5AX
Tel 01422 344344
Printed by Joseph Ward ColourPrint
Dewsbury

A TRUE NORTH BOOK

Copyright © True North Holdings
ISBN: 1 900 463 21 0

£4.99 nett

Contents

Acknowledgments

The publishers would like to thank the following individuals and organisations for their help in the production of this book: the staff of Blackpool Central Library, reference section; Gerry Wolstenholme, football writer and historian; Blackpool Pleasure Beach Limited and Louis Tussauds Waxworks Limited. Thanks are also due to Pauline Bell, Andrew Hales and Mandy Walker for their contributions. Finally, thanks also to the several local businesses who have supported this book and enriched its content with their often fascinating stories.

An icon of Britain, let alone Blackpool, this view of the majestic Tower makes one wonder at the skill and craftsmanship of the men who constructed it over 100 years ago. The impressive steelwork looks robust enough to last for a thousand years - it is impossible to imagine anything causing the removal of the North's best-known landmark from the skyline. Another Blackpool landmark, which was removed from the skyline, was the Great Wheel, pictured here on the right of the Tower. The structure was incredibly advanced and substantial in its day, standing just over 220 feet high.

Around the town centre

Not exactly a picture-postcard view of the resort, but the horizon is unmistakably 'Blackpool', confirmed as being so by the Tower (of course), the white clock tower of the Woolworths store and the pier. Less familiar Blackpool landmarks are seen here; the Gasworks and the old wooden cooling towers of the electricity works. British Railways Central Station is familiar by thousands of holiday makers, but certainly not from this angle. There were around nine steam engines present in the station on the day the scene was captured. This picture was taken, no doubt, to record the construction of the new roof on one of the stands at Blackpool's football club and is thought to date from 1961.

Left: A dramatic scene dating from 1938. It features the construction work taking place to increase the car parking facilities in Blackpool which, in this instance, also provided a coach station below. The Talbot Road Bus Station with overhead multi-storey car-park was completed in 1939 and is remembered for its distinctive cream and green tiles. This cladding corresponded with the colour of the Corporation trams and buses and was considered to be very stylish in its day. It was therefore controversial when, in 1963, the cladding was replaced with grey corrugated steel. Blackpool bucked the trend in depression-hit Britain in the 1930s. Many ambitious building projects were undertaken and it was this decade which saw the introduction of streamlined trams. In addition to the Talbot Road Bus Station construction work created the Casino, the Technical College, Woolworths and the Co-op Emporium. The Derby Baths and the Odeon were also built during this period. It is likely that the work would have continued in the 1940s, but the war years intervened putting further development on hold for a time.

Right: There have been a few changes to Talbot Square since this picture was taken! The most dramatic change has been the removal of the odd-looking spire on the Town Hall building (it was taken down in 1966 after concern was expressed about its ability to remain standing in high winds) and the demise, since this picture was taken, of the elaborate bus and tram shelter which is seen slightly left of centre. The photograph was taken on a bright, but windy afternoon in the early 1950s.

Right: This photograph shows the new Blackpool *Boots* store nearing completion in 1938. Two years earlier the original West Street branch of Boots was destroyed in a terrible fire which claimed the life of one of Blackpool's brave firemen. The new Boots store was to be bigger and better than its predecessor as this impressive picture clearly shows. Building and rebuilding has been an almost constant process in Blackpool throughout the last 100 years and the 1930s, when this work was completed, was no exception. Among the projects undertaken in the '30s were extensions to the Promenade, a new Town Hall Building and Conference Hall, a new pavilion on the North Pier, and the construction of the Derby Baths, which would be opened in May 1940. On the left of this picture the Town Hall spire which rose over 60 feet above the rest of the building can be seen peeping over the roof tops. It is interesting to note that the unusual feature was removed in the mid 1960s because engineers feared that it may collapse under the force of high winds. The Town Hall building featured here dated from 1900 and overlooked Talbot Square.

Left: This picture dates from the mid-1930s and features Lockhart's Cafe. The popular eating place was situated at the junction of Bank Hey Street and Adelaide Street, next door to Hill's Department Store, seen here in the process of being extended. Sadly, Hill's was destroyed in a major fire in the late 1960s.

A view of the Grand Theatre as it was in 1952. The Grand has always had a special place in the hearts of the people of Blackpool, not to mention the thousands of visitors who have enjoyed performances here over the years. The Grand is proud of its reputation as 'the prettiest little theatre in the kingdom' and its long history dating back to 1894 when it was built by the renowned theatre architect Frank Matcham. The opening ceremony took place not long after that for the Tower itself; the theatre had taken nine months to build and cost £20,000.

In recent times the *Grand* had to fight for its survival after the valuable site was earmarked for development by a department store company. The theatre had already been listed as a building of architectural interest - offering some protection from enthusiastic developers. It was around this time, the late 1960s, that the Friends of The Grand organisation was born.

Their success in the struggle to preserve the building and maintain its use as a leading live theatre is well known. The Friends of the Grand raised £250,000 to purchase the theatre in 1980. One of the theatre's finest hours was the re-opening of the 'Glorious Grand' in March 1981 when the Old Vic Company put on their production of "The Merchant of Venice" starring Timothy West and Prunella Scales.

Left: The installation of the escalator at the new Timothy Whites store attracted the crowds. No wonder too, the pre-fabricated construction was massive - notice the size of the curved hand-rails at the top of the escalator compared with the workings below them. All credit to the installation team for managing to carefully push the structure through the narrow opening of the newly-built store. Timothy Whites had stores in virtually every town you could think of. They were a very familiar High Street name as a consequence. The company was later absorbed into the Boots organisation, the Nottingham-based chain of chemists-cum-department stores which enjoys such a great following today. Opposite the construction site was later to become Timothy Whites is the Post Office, and on the other side of the road the Opera House entrance to the Winter Gardens complex.

Right: The steel skeleton for the new Timothy White Store is in place, and the brickwork and other elements of the major project begin to take shape. There is a sharp contrast between the modern, square lines of the brand new building, and the Victorian design of the adjacent property which houses the Refuge Lending Society Ltd. and Chartered Accountants Blane Gaulter and Blane. Motor vehicles always add a touch of nostalgia to a picture like this. The Ford Consul would have been aspired to by many a family motorist in the late 1950s, and the Bedford truck behind it, which saw so much use with the British Army, would have been a similarly popular sight on Britain's roads.

This was the area of Blackpool, in the age before the car became king, where family holidays would begin and end. The grand, canopied entrance to Blackpool Central Station is featured here on a Wakes' Week afternoon in 1952. Here holiday makers would draw their first breath of fresh, Blackpool air as they arrived in the town before setting off to the guest house or hotel to unpack. Departing visitors would pause on the forecourt, for one last look at *Blackpool* before returning to their home town. At the time this picture was taken the train was the preferred method of travel for the majority of visitors to the town. Gradually, motorcars overtook rail transport and this sounded the death knell for the once frantically busy Central Station. Closure followed in 1964 and the land which once hummed with thousands of holiday makers on the busy platforms was turned over to car parking. The actual station building itself was put to use as a bingo hall, a sign of the times which lasted until the structure was pulled down in 1973.

A view looking down Abingdon Road in the early 1960s. It was a cold, crisp day judging by the clothing worn by some of the shoppers in the scene, clutching their shopping bags as they head off into the town centre. The distinctive roof on the tower of Christ Church (Queen's Street) dominates the skyline in the centre of the picture and the Post Office can be seen on the right. Melias and Dewhurst's were popular with shoppers down this street and their premises can be seen further along from the Post Office. A large single-deck VAMBAC tram is shown on the corner, opposite the junction. *VAMBACs* became known as 'Cattle Trucks' by local people, a reference to them being used to transport troops to Rossall Rifle Range during the war. Just before the war, in 1939, 12 of these vehicles had been ordered from English Electric. The characteristic glazed roof on the vehicles later led to them being called 'Sunliners.' Just as a matter of interest, the tram livery with green above the 'waistline' and cream below it was introduced in 1958.

Left: Work is underway here on the site which later to become the location of British Home Stores. This photograph was taken in 1955. Prior to the construction work the area was used as an open-air market place with adjacent Market Hall and Market Hotel. Car parking spaces were provided alongside the market area. The West Street multi-storey car park would more than compensate for the loss of the parking spaces previously available, and this structure went up at the same time as the BHS store. The opening of BHS took place in a ceremony held in 1957.

Right: Winifred Street was the location of this 1964 view, and in the background the Albert Street carpark can be seen under construction. It could have been one of half a dozen pictures of concrete multistory car parking facilities in the process of growing out of the once bustling back streets at this time. The reason was simple enough - as car ownership increased it took over from rail travel as the preferred method of transport into Blackpool. An overwhelming proportion of the millions of visitors to the resort would now arrive by car and it was obvious to everyone that additional space was needed to accommodate them. The increasing number of day trippers, also attributable to the growing ownership and use of motorcars, added to the problem (or *opportunity*) depending on which side of the counter you were standing. The decline in rail users also resulted in a reduction in rail facilities in the town. Central Station, the starting point for many an enjoyable family holiday, closed in November 1964. With 14 platforms and associated services to match, it had served the town since 1863. Ironically the track bed became the route for a new, fast road into Blackpool, and the cleared site where the once proud and immensely busy station stood, became a parking area for cars and coaches.

Right: This quiet Blackpool scene shows Abingdon Street from Talbot Road and dates from 1952. Two buildings dominate the view; the domed roof of the Winter Gardens and *Her Majesty's Opera House.* The first ever Royal Variety Performance to take place outside London was staged here, in April 1955. On the left of the scene St. John's Church dominates the skyline behind the building housing the Post Office and the market area.

A visit to the area today reveals that some of the property on the left of the photograph has been pulled down in the developments which have taken over the last thirty years or so and is now replaced by modern shop units. This is a quieter district now than the hustle and bustle which continues relentlessly, during *the season* at least, just a hundred yards away. Such is the nature of Blackpool.

Left: The crowds turned out to see Father Christmas when he visited Blackpool in the 1940s, to be drawn through the town on his sleigh by a team of ponies. The picture also affords a rare view of Blackpool North Railway Station. The first Blackpool North railway station was situated on Dickson Road and was the entry point for the thousands of holiday makers who visited the resort from its earliest beginnings. It was rebuilt at the turn of the century, but cleared completely to make way for a supermarket in the mid-70s. Modern rail travellers arrive at the sleek, new *Blackpool North* which first served the town in April 1974.

In this picture atmosphere is generated by the excited looks on the childrens' faces as they watch Father Christmas leave the station precincts. Happy days!

This is how the corner of Abingdon Street appeared around forty years ago, retail activity revolving around the ladies' outfitters trading under the name of G.E Wilcock. The shop is of an unusual design with elements of the frontage being added after it was first constructed. The buildings in this area date from a little after the middle of the last century. Trams no longer run along this road and the site shown here is now occupied by the Job Centre, just across the road from Blackpool's Central Library. The photograph is known to date from 1959; the eve of the birth of *the sixties*, a time which would see Blackpool rise to the challenge of the changing needs of holiday makers with a degree of success which left rival resorts breathless.

Were it not for the bold lettering denoting the location of Lewis's Blackpool store it would take more than a moment or two to work out where this scene was set. The photograph is dramatic in as much as it shows the terrific contrast between the ant-like figures on the seafront, the Dinky-style cars and the huge monolith that was the Lewis's store. Lewis's was built upon the site of the Palace Theatre; in turn, The Palace was formerly the Blackpool Alhambra, a popular place of entertainment with 2,800 seats dating back to 1897. This photograph was taken around five years after Lewis's had first opened its doors in April 1964. The well known retailer provided a valuable service from this location for just less than 30 years, finally closing in 1993. The distinctive honeycomb exterior was removed after the store closed, and extensive alterations took place (including reducing the height of the building by two floors) before it was opened as a Woolworths store in 1994.

A major entertainment venue in Blackpool, certain to be remembered with fondness by thousands of visitors to the town, was the Queen's Theatre. The venue was situated at the western end of Hounds Hill and had almost 1700 seats and three licensed bars. The building began life as the Borough Theatre in September 1877 and was later to be known as Feldman's, named after the successful music publisher, Bertram Feldman, but it was sold in 1952 and re-named *Queen's* from that time. 1938 saw an extensive renovation of the premises and the addition of many art-deco features. The building was pulled down to make way for a new C&A department store.

These smiles must have been quite an effort, especially where the adults are concerned, when the press photographer turned up to record their misery. This picture appeared in many of the national papers, showing Blackpool as very few people had seen it during terrible flooding in 1963. We can't help but smile a little ourselves, at the lack of self-consciousness evident here, in the people with their rolled-up trousers. The gentleman outside Mr. Wilcock's fish and chip shop looks particularly spooky! It is easy to be light hearted about the people in the picture, and it *is* over thirty years ago, but let's hope that the householders in this street managed to clear up the terrible mess and return to normal life with the minimum of bother.

From the promenade to the beach

The appearance of the entertainment complex beneath the Tower has changed dramatically over the years. This is how it looked in 1953, when Freddie Platt and the Tower Band wooed appreciative audiences in the Tower Ballroom. Three years after this photograph was taken, in December 1956, a disastrous fire gutted the ballroom. It was renovated at a cost of £500,000 - a huge amount of money at the time, but the finished effect really was one of the *wonders* of Blackpool. The beautiful ceiling in the ballroom had 2000 square feet of hand painted murals across its 120 ft length. Of course, in terms of entertainment, Blackpool was more famous for Reginald Dixon's organ music than anything else.

The resort's best-loved entertainer earned his living at the mighty Wurlitzer organ over a 40 year period between 1930 and 1970. On his retirement, marked by a special, sell-out concert on BBC radio, he received goodwill messages from show business's greatest stars from all over the world. In this scene from almost half a century ago, The Palace Theatre can be seen on the site which was once occupied by the Prince of Wales Theatre. The Palace made its name and built its reputation in the days of *Music Hall*. Many of the country's leading performers appeared here. Eventually the theatre became part of the Blackpool Tower Company, and later still was integrated into the *First Leisure* organisation. It was sold in 1962 and pulled down to make way for the Lewis's store. In recent years the Lewis's building was 'restyled' and the distinctive honeycomb-effect facade removed to enable Woolworths to run their busy store from this location.

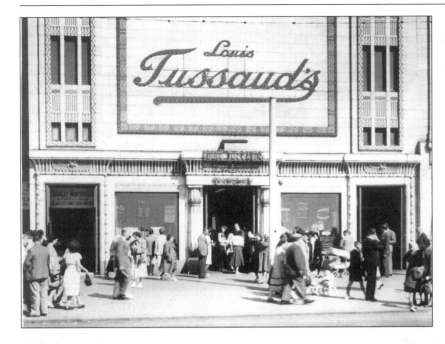

Below: It is difficult to appreciate the sheer size of the task which faced the engineers who built Blackpool Tower at the end of the last century. The undertaking would be challenging enough in modern times, but when one imagines the lack of resources from heavy lifting gear down to powered hand-tools it is amazing that the structure was ever built at all. Against this background it is surprising that the people associated with actually constructing the Tower are not at all well known. The firm of architects was Maxwell and Tukes of Manchester and the consultant engineer was Mr. R. J. G Read of Westminster. Construction work on the Tower itself was undertaken by Mr. W. Bell and Mr. J. Wilcox and the construction firm credited with the work was Heenan and Froude Ltd. of Worcester. Remarkably the Tower was first opened to visitors in 1894, only three years after the foundation stone was laid.

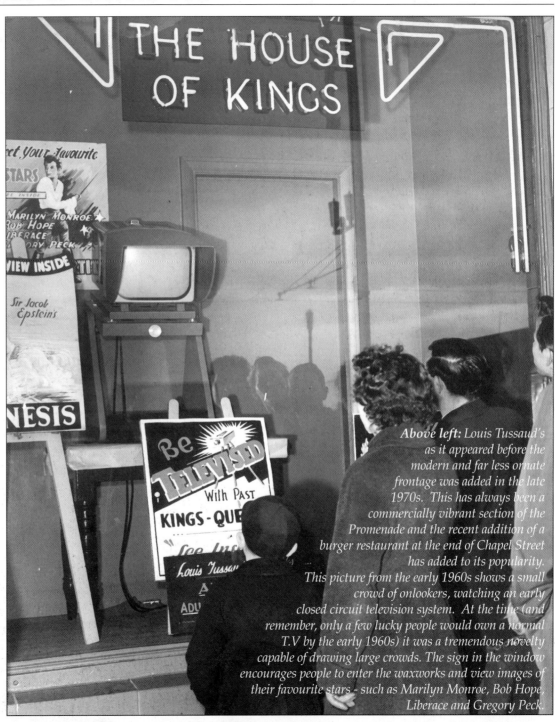

Above left: Louis Tussaud's as it appeared before the modern and far less ornate frontage was added in the late 1970s. This has always been a commercially vibrant section of the Promenade and the recent addition of a burger restaurant at the end of Chapel Street has added to its popularity.
This picture from the early 1960s shows a small crowd of onlookers, watching an early closed circuit television system. At the time (and remember, only a few lucky people would own a normal T.V by the early 1960s) it was a tremendous novelty capable of drawing large crowds. The sign in the window encourages people to enter the waxworks and view images of their favourite stars - such as Marilyn Monroe, Bob Hope, Liberace and Gregory Peck.

Left: The crowds turned out to see the Maria Noble, Blackpool's new lifeboat, when she was displayed outside the lifeboat station in 1961. She replaced the *Sara Ann Austin* and was also a *Liverpool* class vessel of just over 35ft in length. Maria Noble had more modern fittings, including two 20 h.p. diesel engines. The vessel was originally based in Exmouth and had already achieved a total of 35 lives saved since it entered service there in 1953. In June 1963 the Maria Noble was involved in an unusual accident whilst in the process of being launched. This involved being pushed out of the Lifeboat Station by the launching tractor, to be turned around and towed down the slipway to the shore. During the operation to push the Maria Noble out of the station she hit a passing tramcar, damaging the roof and causing a shower of glass to fall on the shocked passengers. Thankfully, nobody was hurt and the incident caused only a short delay in launching the lifeboat. *Maria Noble* served Blackpool until her replacement, the *Edgar Orlando and Eva Child* arrived in 1970.

Right: Situated beside the Central Pier, opposite Blackpool's waxworks, the lifeboat station goes almost unnoticed by the hundreds of thousands of people who walk past it each season. The station dates back to 1937, when it was officially opened by H.R.H The Duke of Kent. The Duke had the honour of naming the new lifeboat "Sara Ann Austin" and opened Victoria Hospital and the newly-built North Promenade during the same visit. The new lifeboat was a 35ft 6ins *Liverpool* class weighing 7 tons and crewed by a team of 7. The vessel had a single, petrol-driven engine capable of generating 35 horse power and cost just short of £4,000 to build. The *Sarah Ann Austin* guarded the Blackpool coastline until 1960. She was last launched on Whit Sunday in June of that year after a sudden, violent storm took holiday makers on the crowded beaches by surprise. The alarm was raised when someone reported a sighting of a person drifting out to sea on an airbed, and the lifeboat was launched. In the event the report proved to be false, though not malicious.

A tranquil scene showing the North Promenade in 1952. Part of the appeal of Blackpool when this scene was recorded was the fresh sea air. Remember that many of the resort's visitors lived in the Yorkshire and Lancashire mill towns where the air was thick with pollution from scores of mill chimneys. The North Shore area provided a welcome contrast to the hustle and bustle of Blackpool's more commercial area, with plenty of broad walking space where couples could chat and relax during their holiday. The tower in the centre of this photograph housed a lift which took passengers up and down the cliff face, between the front and the boating pool beneath it. The fully-enclosed boating pool was an impressive structure with a sturdy, curved sea wall. Here, parents could relax beside the pool in the sunshine, mindful of the fact that their children were safe and fully occupied in the water before them.

Main picture: The original caption for this photograph was "Donkey man." It refers to the plight of the man offering donkey rides in the centre left of the picture. Thousands of holiday makers and eager children would have been potential customers for the rides, but the poor man was so hemmed-in by the mass of bodies that he was unable to exploit the demand! The photograph dates from the 1930s, and the difference between 'than' and 'now' is amazing. People here seem even less litter-conscious than they do in the 1990s, if the scattered papers on the edge of the beach are anything to go by. It looks like quite a warm day, yet most of the adult men and some of the children are wearing jackets and *ties!* On the left of the picture a giant mock tea pot is offering holiday makers jugs of tea, and next to that about ten beach huts provide the chance to get changed (into the one-piece bathing suits which were so popular) before taking to the sea.

On the Promenade about twenty trams, of various shapes and sizes, appear to be bringing even more people to the beach.... though goodness only knows where they would all sit!

Left: A contrast to the main photograph on this page, in as much as it shows a rare view of the deserted beach with the older-style and, as yet, undeveloped properties in the background. The picture was taken by a well-known Blackburn professional photographer, Wally Talbot who gave it the title "Lone Sailor, No Ships." It dates from 1955 and was circulated to many national newspapers for publicity purposes.

White knuckles!

BY GUM! BUT WE SHOULD MAKE A MESS
IF WE MISSED THIS HOLE

ON THE REEL AT THE PLEASURE BEACH, BLACKPOOL

We all have memories of the Fun House; as children we were all too eager to get inside and experience the many strange effects of our minds and bodies as we made our way through the various obstacles. Later, as parents, many of us have enjoyed re-living our childhood through the experiences of our own children. This was the largest Fun House in the world when it opened in 1934, containing more than 50 different and exciting 'experiences' inside. The figure of the laughing man, with his infectious, uncontrollable chuckling, was perhaps, the most memorable feature of this part of the Pleasure Beach. It had entertained visitors to Blackpool on this spot since 1935. Sadly a devastating fire destroyed the Fun House in 1991.

All photographs in this section by kind permission of Blackpool Pleasure Beach Ltd.

Above: A very proud party poses beside an aeroplane in this picture from 1935. Business was obviously booming for the Pleasure Beach when Leonard Thompson, the managing director of the day, chartered this Imperial Airways Horatius to fly from Squires Gate to Brussels. The occasion was the opening of the new International Exposition in Brussels, for which the Pleasure Beach management team had been asked to construct an amusement park. Senior staff from Blackpool and several local dignitaries were flown out on the chartered 'plane to view their success and celebrate the achievement. More publicity for the Big Dipper, the greatest contribution that Mr. Strickler made to Blackpool pleasure Beach, was achieved by this picture postcard from 1924. The high, sweeping curve of the ride as shown here may have looked somewhat exaggerated when compared to the dimensions of the real thing, but the simple drawing brilliantly succeeds in capturing the excitement of the ride. At the time the *Big Dipper* would have been just as intriguing, mysterious and captivating as the *Big-One* later became. The future would see the two rides running closely together, some 70 years after this image was created. Right and facing page: 1930s postcard promoting the *Big Dipper* and the *Reel.*

IF YOU'VE GOT THE "PIP" TRY THE "BIG DIP" AT THE PLEASURE BEACH BLACKPOOL

This aerial view of the Pleasure Beach dates from 1935. The Promenade borders the left-hand side of the picture and the Casino can be seen at the top left corner. The right hand side of the Pleasure Beach is 'framed' by the impressive structure which is the Big Dipper. Maxim's Flying Machine can clearly be seen, as can Noah's Ark, the Boating Pool and the Indian Theatre. This view really shows how much the facilities had developed since the Pleasure Beach was born. The comprehensive entertainment afforded by the vast array of rides and attractions would guarantee the future success of Blackpool's biggest crowd-puller.

Right: Six people lost their lives in October 1927 when flooding brought devastation to the Fylde coast. It is said that a huge tidal wave was caused by hurricane-force winds combining with the high tide. The Pleasure Beach did not escape the onslaught, as can be seen here; the route up to the Casino looks more akin to Venice than Blackpool, and it was several days before the attractions were able to clean up and get back to normal. The year before this picture was taken saw the opening of the South Promenade by Lord Derby. To achieve this, scores of acres of sand dunes were reclaimed and a wide road with separate tramway was built.

Left: Fire has been the scourge of many fine attractions and buildings in Blackpool over the years. From piers to theatres, the flames have done considerable damage to the resort's favourite places - and even Blackpool Tower has not escaped fire damage over the years.
This picture shows the untimely demise of the Indian Theatre in September 1939.

Right: And royalty came too. The Duke and Duchess of Gloucester were the Pleasure Beach's first official royal visitors when they arrived in April 1976 and travelled around and above the park on the Monorail.

Left: A photograph from 1923 - over 70 years ago - shows the intricate lattice-work which made up the frame of the Big Dipper. It was the first "woodie" at the Pleasure Beach to use special under-track friction wheels, allowing the design to incorporate steeper descents and sharper bends on the course. The size of the ride can only be appreciated when you compare it to the relatively small figures in the three cars coming towards the camera. Interestingly, the sandy beach is shown coming right up to the foot of the Big Dipper in this picture, but at the time the scene was captured the new promenade had driven the sea back more than a hundred yards to the West.

Blackpool at war

This picture dates from 1939 and features the construction of a public air-raid shelter on the Promenade. Compared to some neighbouring towns and cities Blackpool escaped relatively lightly in terms of bomb damage. There was always the danger that the town would attract stray bombers shedding their loads after an unsuccessful sortie to one of the large adjacent industrial areas. Similarly, Blackpool was a major centre for wartime service training in its own right, and consequently was at considerable risk. Of course, air raid shelters were being built throughout the whole of the country at this time, and many hours would be spent huddled together in them over the course of the next six years.

The caption on the back of this photograph reads 'Battle For France Exhibition - 1944.' During the last war there were dozens of 'promotional' fund-raising events throughout Britain, including War Weapons Week, Warship Week, Wings For Victory Week and various re-cycling 'weeks' to encourage people to donate cash and all manner of recyclable household items which could be turned into weapons to be directed towards the enemy. Blackpool played an almost unique role in wartime Britain. It also brought challenges and opportunities which were met and exploited in true Blackpool style. There was a massive military presence in the town throughout the war. Almost three quarters of a million

Blackpool Football Club

The War-time Blackpool side line up for a minute's silence in tribute to ex-team mate William Wilfred (Billy) Parr who was a sergeant-pilot killed in an RAF training accident on 10 March 1942. This tribute took place before the game against Stoke City on 28 March when the Blackpool team, from left to right, was Dodds, captain, Roxburgh, Johnston, Williams, Finan, Mortensen, Whittaker, O'Donnell, Matthews, Pope and Powell. Blackpool won 4-0 with goals from O'Donnell and three from the incomparable Jock Dodds, who went on to score an incredible 65 goals in 30 games during that season. Of these players, only Dodds, Roxburgh, Johnston, Finan and Mortensen were officially Blackpool players, the remainder were guest players, servicemen stationed in the town who played when they were available. The War thus brought together, arguably, Blackpool's greatest ever side as they won the Northern Section championship three years in succession, 1941/42, 1942/43 and 1943/44 and in addition won the War Cup knock-out competition in 1942/43, were runners-up in 1943/44 and defeated Arsenal in a north versus south Challenge Cup Final played at Stamford Bridge on 15 May 1943. Billy Parr, an amateur international whilst with Blackpool, had to request time off from his official duties at the Corporation Cleansing Department in order to play for the club. He had moved to London in November 1938 to take up a post at the Wembley Council offices but he was remembered with affection by the club and regularly called in at Bloomfield Road when he came home to Blackpool to visit his family.

Most of the training at Blackpool Football Club was done at Bloomfield Road in the 1940 and 1950 era rather than at any special training ground. There were plenty of laps of the track, a little exercise with the ball and, for those who needed to strengthen their legs after an injury, there was even running up and down the terraces of the Spion Kop!

Here, lapping on the west side of the ground, are (left to right) Eddie Shimwell, Stan Mortensen, George Dick, Jimmy McIntosh, partly hidden, Joe Robinson, Ronnie Suart, Hughie Kelly, partly hidden, Stan Matthews, Harry Johnston, Walter Rickett, Eric Hayward and, bringing up the rear, Alec Munro.

The players are training prior to Blackpool's first appearance in an FA Cup Final when they took on Manchester United at Wembley on 24 April 1948. Ronnie Suart, left back and later manager of the club, was injured in a game against Sunderland on 12 April and missed out; his place was taken by the relatively unknown Johnny Crosland, who up to that point had only played two first team games during the season. Also missing from the Cup Final line-up was Jimmy McIntosh, who had played in all the previous rounds. The forward line was reshuffled and his place in the side was taken by Walter Rickett.

Blackpool lost a memorable final 4-2 but, ironically, just four days later the two clubs met again at Bloomfield Road in a League game and Mortensen's goal gave Blackpool a 1-0 win. Jimmy McIntosh returned for that game and also for the final game of the season at Preston and scored five goals in Blackpool's record away victory, a 7-0 thrashing of the old enemy.

Above: An almost full Bloomfield Road, 29,128 inside, on 10 September 1938 when Aston Villa were the visitors; in those days through to the mid 1950s, Blackpool regularly attracted 25-35,000 spectators with the packed Spion Kop (left of the photograph) being the focal point for home supporters. The record attendance at Bloomfield Road is 38,098 on 17 September 1955 for the visit of Wolverhampton Wanderers who were beaten 2-1 with goals from Mortensen and Matthews.

The Spion Kop was originally just a gravel mound but for the club's entry into the First Division in 1930/31 it was developed into "a hill made predominantly out of cinders and sand, packed together with railway sleepers". And for the opening game, Arsenal attracted a record crowd at the ground, 27,694 paying £1,896 for the privilege. The mighty Arsenal also brought record crowds in the following two seasons with 29,576 in 1931 and 30,218 in 1932. Leicester City very nearly emulated the Arsenal feat, attracting record crowds in 1936, 30,759, and 1937, 31,783.

The Kop was concreted and terraced during the close season of 1950 and this brought the Bloomfield Road capacity up to the mid 30,000s. Sadly, with very few changes, the ground can now only accommodate just over 11,000 with the once great Kop reduced, for safety reasons, to around 1,400 for away supporters only. But there is a new ground in the offing at a site, Whyndyke Farm, on the outskirts of the town where the capacity is expected to be anything between 20,000 and 40,000.

Right: In the halcyon days of the 1950s and 1960s, even the Blackpool reserve side flew to the occasional away fixture. Here the Blackpool party are on the steps of a Silver City Airways Dakota DC 3 at Squires Gate airport prior to their departure for a reserve game at Newcastle on 26 March 1960. The players are, left to right, Gordon West, still only a young amateur, Roy Fawcett, Ean Cuthbert, Leslie Lea, Brian Tyrell, Peter Smethurst, Glyn James, Jack Duckworth (trainer), Peter

Hauser, Hughie Kelly and on the steps Stephen 'Mandy' Hill, Tommy Garrett, Bruce Crawford and David Jones. Garrett and Tyrell, an Irishman who never made the first team, were travelling as reserves; the side lost 4-2 with goals from Bruce Crawford, whose father, Bobby, had played for Blackpool in the early 1930s, and Peter Smethurst West, an England Youth international, later signed for Everton for £27,500 a then-record transfer fee for a goalkeeper, Lea played in European competitions for Cardiff City before finishing his career with Barnsley, Hill won England Under 23 caps and Glyn James became club captain, playing over 400 games and won nine Welsh international caps before becoming a successful local businessman.

The Blackpool team pose with the FA Cup,. won on a dramatic day in May 1953 when Bolton Wanderers were beaten 4-3, having led 3-1 with 35 minutes left for play. The final was dubbed 'The Matthews Final' but Stan himself decrys this with "I say we had eleven match-winners" and points out that it was the other Stan, Mortensen, who scored three of Blackpool's goals. The players, left to right, are back row: Eddie Shimwell, Harry Johnston, George

FOOTBALL ASSOCIATION
CHALLENGE CUP FINAL
1953

BLACKPOOL
versus
BOLTON WANDERERS

DINNER
AT THE
CAFÉ ROYAL
REGENT STREET, LONDON, W.1
SATURDAY, MAY 2nd, 1953

Farm, Johnny Crosland, Cyril Robinson, Allan Brown; middle row: Joe Smith (manager), Stan Matthews, Ernie Taylor, Stan Mortensen, Jackie Mudie, Bill Perry, Johnny Lynas, (trainer); front row: Ewan Fenton, George McKnight, Hughie Kelly, Tommy Garrett. Allan Brown missed out on his second Cup Final appearance through injury, Hughie Kelly was also out injured and McKnight and Crosland were spectators at Wembley, having played in previous rounds. A young Cyril Robinson, who had previously only played two first team games, was given his chance at left half. After the Final the players attended a celebration dinner at the Café Royal in Regent Street where there was Creme Germiny, Delice de Sole Cardinale, Poulet de Surrey Grand-Mere and Soufflé en Surprise Milady on offer, the latter presumably named after the local firm Waller & Hartley whose trade name was Milady. The toasts were for 'Her Majesty the Queen', "The Blackpool Football Club', The Football Association and The Football League' and 'Our Guests', proposed by Blackpool's Vice-Chairman Albert Hindley and responded to by Ivan Sharpe, journalist and one time Olympic gold medal winner.

their away games during this period.

The celebratory journey took in the whole of the Fylde Coast from Squires Gate to Cleveleys and ended, around five o'clock, on the steps of the Town hall where 15,000 fans were waiting to greet their heroes. The first arrivals had queued since 11 o'clock in the morning and had been entertained by the British Legion Band. Cinema and newsreel cameras had followed the coach on its journey and TV and BBC radio microphones had been set up to record the scenes in Talbot Square.

Prior to an official reception inside the Town Hall the Mayor, Councillor Peter Fairhurst JP, welcomed the team home and added "The reception which you have just received now and on your tour of the town is some proof of the tremendous admiration we all have for your magnificent effort at Wembley. We hope that now the Cup has been brought to Blackpool it will, in years to come, become a constant visitor to the town." Sadly for Seasiders' fans, it has never returned to date!

On their return from the Wembley triumph of 1953, the Blackpool team were greeted by thousands of fans who lined the streets to welcome them home. Here the players, Fenton, Johnston, Mortensen, Matthews, Taylor, Garrett and Perry, display the FA Cup to their admirers along the Promenade, just south of West Street. The building at the extreme right of the photograph is Collinsons Grill and Coffee where many of the players met after training for a cup of coffee and a chat whilst W Lyons was, as the wording on the blind implies, an exclusive dress shop. The coach on which they arc riding is one belonging to Seagull Coaches, a firm who regularly transported the Blackpool players to

Bird's eye view

A picture postcard aerial view of Blackpool Tower taken from the south. Three landmarks dominate the scene; the Tower, standing almost 519 feet above the shore line and weighing nearly 4,000 tons; the magnificent North Pier, originally constructed to allow people to experience a bracing walk above the waves; and finally the white curved facade of the Woolworths building, complete with clock tower and popular restaurant.

The area behind the tower was destined to be cleared in later years. British Home Stores and the West Street carpark would be created here in the late 1950s and the Lewis's department store constructed on the site of the Palace Theatre in the early 1960s. Blackpool has always tried to strike a successful balance between the needs of its residents, the obvious need to maintain its leading position as a top tourist centre, and the difficult task of competing with the major retail developments in other nearby Lancashire towns and cities. Major retailers are attracted to Blackpool by the tremendous numbers of visitors to the town, but their changing requirements over the years have resulted in considerable disruption to local folk as new buildings have come and gone.

This aerial photograph was taken looking across the Promenade from a height of 300 feet. On the bottom right of the picture we can just make out the end of the South Pier, and read the lettering on the sign above it. The 928 ft South Pier was originally known as the Victoria Pier when it opened in 1893. Many considered it to be the best of Blackpool's piers right up until its name was changed in 1930. During the Second World War the RAF used the pier and in 1958 it was destroyed in a devastating fire. The road which leads away from the camera, at right angles to the Promenade, is Station Road, the broad thoroughfare linking the sea front with Lytham Road. Though not visible here, the South Shore open air baths stood adjacent to the South Pier, on its right. In later years this site was to be taken over by the Sandcastle leisure complex. On the left of this picture we can see two or three large Victorian properties at the side of the Promenade. Many would, of course, find use as boarding houses and small hotels over the years; others would sell a variety of products from what was once the garden or yard in front of the property. As the popularity of Blackpool grew there was an irresistible incentive to turn over the forecourt areas along the front to commercial use in order to satisfy the demands for everything from ice creams to *kiss me quick* hats.

Away from the crowds we see another side to Blackpool. The character which initially made the resort attractive to Lancashire's very first holiday makers and visitors, one which had more to do with relaxation and reflection than the buzz and excitement of the Golden Mile, the theatres and cinemas, the Pleasure Beach and amusement arcades. In modern times this part of Blackpool is valued and treasured by more mature visitors, and those looking for a place to recharge their batteries and get away from the hustle and bustle of modern life. For here, on the northern end of the resort, the emphasis has always been on *promenading*, pleasant invigorating walks along the sea front, being pampered in large hotels such as the Imperial and The Norbreck, the healing powers of sea water and time spent with loved ones which would create lasting memories.

Blackpool Pleasure Beach as few people have ever seen it. The view was captured from a 'plane flying at 500 ft in the summer of 1948. The coach park can be seen at the top right of the picture and many familiar rides, including the *Grand National* and *Sir Hiram Maxim's Captive Flying Machine* in the centre of the picture. Hiram Maxim was the man who invented the Maxim Machine Gun. The Pleasure Beach developed from the South Shore fairground which had occupied this site since well before the turn of the century. The Pleasure Beach, as we know it, owes much to one Mr. Bean. This visionary had nothing in common with the bumbling comedian we are familiar with today; he was W G Bean, a Londoner who arrived in Blackpool in 1896 with the idea of setting up an American-style amusement park in the town. The rest is history, for the Pleasure Beach became one of Blackpool's biggest and most popular crowd pullers, known throughout the world.

The building seen at the top left of this photograph is the Casino, dating from 1939. It replaced an even more elaborate Casino building was had stood at the same location since 1919 and served millions of visitors as a restaurant and theatre.

A tower-top view of the Central Station with the domestic rooftops and the gas works in the distance. The photograph dates from 1908, making the view almost a century old. The picture gives some impression of the blackness caused by the smoke from countless domestic chimneys, not to mention the funnels of the railway engines as they haul their trains in and out of the station. It is impossible to overestimate the influence that the railway had on the development of Blackpool. The railway came to Poulton in 1840, joining it with Preston. This made Blackpool more accessible to the masses, with coaches (horse drawn of course!) being employed by the hotels to complete the last four miles of the journey. In April 1846 a branch line from Poulton to Talbot Road was completed and the means for cheap, mass travel into Blackpool was established. This was over 150 years ago, and the growth of Blackpool since that time has been phenomenal. Over the years that followed, travel by car became a more popular method of access to the resort, and the opening of the M55 motorway in 1975 caused a substantial increase in the number of day trippers.

At your leisure

Below: A pleasant hour or two could be passed by audiences at various beauty competitions. This young lady was an entrant in a 1930s 'beautiful hair' contest. These were often held at the South Shore Open Air Baths and several other locations at the resort. They served to take the monotony out of sun bathing sessions, and to give young hopefuls the chance to get into the limelight and get 'noticed' by their peers. Often, events like these would be attended by freelance photographers, and the Blackpool publicity machine was well served when, throughout the summer, pictures like this one found their way onto the pages of local newspapers throughout the land.

Left: June 1923 saw the opening of the South Shore Open Air Baths. The splendid new public attraction cost a considerable, at the time, £70,000 and was modelled on Rome's Colosseum. Not that many visitors to 1920s Blackpool would have seen the famous monument to Roman architecture of course. This crowded scene shows the stately pillars and domed roof of the classical cafe and entrance hall. Before the end of the 1920s over four million visitors had sampled the delights of the open air baths, said to be the largest open-air bathing facility in the world. Bathing beauty contests were popular well attended events at the South Shore Open Air Baths, and afternoon mannequin parades would regularly take place, with attractive young ladies showing off the latest fashions available at local stores. In addition there were 'aquatic displays' performed by Blackpool Amateur Swimming Club, much to the appreciation of the lazy, sun-drenched audience.

Sadly, the 1960s heralded a decline in the popularity of the South Shore Pool. By 1983 the facility was pulled down and replaced by an indoor swimming pool with a whole host of modern features and ancillary services designed to attract the crowds.

Above: Jimmy Edwards was a favourite children's entertainer in the 1960s. This picture was taken in 1963 when the 'Professor' had just completed his judging duties at the South Shore Open Air Baths. Jimmy Edwards was famous for his television series 'Whacko' and he was also a popular entertainer with Blackpool audiences. The lady doing the 'tweeking' of the famous Edwards moustache was Miss Val Martin of Blackburn. Val later went on to win the Miss Great Britain contest.

Right: Blackpool has, for a long time, been associated with all things beautiful. These gorgeous young ladies epitomise Blackpool bathing beauties at their best and are seen enjoying the attention in the aftermath of a contest at the South Shore Open Air Baths. The picture dates from 1959 and features the winner of *Miss Blackpool 1959* and the two runners up. They all look delightful as they pose for the camera with one of the judges. The man in question was no less than Edmund Hockeridge, the bass-baritone crooner who enjoyed phenomenal success in the 1950s and '60s. The good-looking vocalist had a voice to match and went on to achieve great success and many television appearances.

This photograph would make an ideal picture for a caption competition! We know that it dates from around 1960 and that it depicts a childrens outing organised by the Blackpool Taxi Operators Association. The two cars seen in here are Vauxhall Crestas, stylish, spacious, wallowing family saloons, influenced by the design of American cars of the day. They were ideally suited for use as taxis. The celebrity attraction at the event was the gentleman pictured alongside the Mayor of Blackpool. Most readers over the age of 40 will recognise him as being 'Mr Pastry' - real name Richard Hearne. His appearance, resembling a cross between Charlie Chaplin and Dad's Army's Corporal Jones, went down a storm with children in his day, and he became on of the first childrens' entertainers to achieve tremendous popularity through television.

The Grand Theatre - prettiest in the land

The Grand Theatre, reputed to be the prettiest little theatre in the kingdom, is situated right at the heart of Blackpool's busy town centre. Built by the famous theatre architect, Frank Matcham, in 1894, the Grand has had an interesting and eventful history.

It was owned originally by Thomas Sergenson who came to Blackpool in 1876 to be Treasurer of the Prince of Wales Theatre. He went on successfully to lease several theatres in the town, but his dream was to to build his very own full sized theatre in Blackpool on the most modern principles.

In October 1887, he bought a block of old property on the corner of Church Street and St. Ann Street (now Corporation Street). This was a first class position between the Winter Gardens and the Promenade, on one of the best shopping streets in Blackpool. He announced that, in 1888, he would start to build his new Grand Theatre, together with five shops. The rent from the shops would allow him to run the new theatre at no more than he paid for his existing Blackpool leases.

Meanwhile, the Winter Gardens Company decided to build an Opera House designed by the eminent theatre architect, Frank Matcham, to be opened on June 10th 1889. Sergenson thought he should build only the five shops on his site until he could see how the rival Opera House prospered.

In place of his theatre, Sergenson erected a large wooden building with a corrugated iron roof and opened on July 11th 1889 with Ohmy's Circus. The following year, a portion of the theatre wall was built and the circus erected inside it. Then, in 1891, the foundation stone for the Blackpool Tower was laid. Due to open in the spring of 1894, Sergenson, owner of the temporary Ohmy Grand Circus, saw at once that the sophisticated Tower Circus meant the end of his little enterprise.

He therefore decided to press on with the completion of his half-built theatre in Church Street, and commissioned Frank Matcham to design "the best, prettiest and cosiest theatre possible." In 1894, the Grand Theatre and Opera House duly opened, a few weeks after the Tower itself and Sergenson immediately christened his theatre 'Matcham's Masterpiece'. It had cost £20,000 and had taken nine months to build.

Following the opening, the Grand flourished and Thomas Sergenson sold his theatre to the Blackpool Tower Company. The Grand Theatre became a major venue on the touring circuit, with all the leading actors of the day playing there. It became a thriving home for the best in entertainment and the summer variety shows frequently broke records. In 1967 the EMI company bought out the Tower Company and wanted to sell the theatre site for building. Fortunately it had already become a listed building for its architectural interest. Because of this scare, the Friends of the Grand was formed, a small group of local people who are still struggling to preserve their heritage to this day.

The theatre closed in 1972. At the public enquiry the following year the case went in favour of the theatre as it was deemed to have a role in Blackpool's civic and commercial life, but no shows materialised.

The Friends of the Grand formed themselves into a limited company with charitable status and, after a compromise was reached with the authorities in 1977, EMI restored the theatre, dramatically and beautifully on the understanding that the Friends, now the Blackpool Grand Theatre Trust Limited, would not oppose bingo on the premises.

The Trust was given an option to buy the theatre for £350,000, the cost later reduced to £250,000. The Trust meanwhile had a limited use of the theatre and many artistes supported efforts to raise money.

Finally, in 1980, with help from various organisations the theatre was bought.

Teams of volunteers got it ready for a triumphant production of 'The Merchant of Venice' which was attended by the Prince of Wales

The theatre now offers an exciting and varied programme including visits from top opera, theatre and ballet companies. A major award from the National Lottery in 1996 improved facilities and helped to develop the Studio Theatre. A hundred years old now, the theatre is looking forward to a second successful century.

Right and facing page, far left: Two early programmes advertising the acts. Facing page, centre: The foyer as seen at the turn of the century. Facing page, right: The theatre from around the same period. Above, centre: An advertising promotion from the 1920s. Left: The theatre as seen from the stage.

The Grand Theatre, 33 Church Street, Blackpool FY1 1HT

Box Office: 01253 290190

Working life

Right: No prizes for guessing what the weather was like outside when this photograph was taken! Raincoats in abundance were an indication of a wet day which had driven Blackpool holiday makers off the beach and into the *Nalgo* exhibition seen here. The photograph dates from 1946 and a variety of products and services are being shown off at the Corporation-sponsored event. To the modern eye it all appears a bit haphazard, not to say disorganised, and the choice of exhibits seems a bit strange. At the bottom left of the picture there is a stand displaying bus engines and electric motors from trams. Towards the centre of the exhibition items relating to trams, such as the poles for collecting the electric current and various switching devices can be seen. The centrepiece of the show is the working model of the tramway and bus network which even includes details of how the money spent on the public transport service is broken down into categories.

Part of the exhibition is given over to 'Health' and in the first year after the end of the Second World War this was a subject that the country was beginning to get to grips with. Just two years later the National Health Service was formed in Britain, and despite very difficult economic conditions, a drive began to improve every aspect of public health, from housing and sanitation, to major issues such as air quality. Another part of the exhibition is given over to 'Gas' with an almost full size model of a street lamp and various other domestic appliances on display.

Facing page, larger picture: Another view of the 1946 exhibition. It seems that the highlight of the day for the three lads in the centre of the picture was having their picture taken. Poor things, apart from the giant tram and bus set in the middle of the hall there was precious little to keep their minds busy at this gathering. Still, it would have been slightly better than dodging the rain drops outside... and a lot better than being at school!

Left: "Who sold you this then..?" could be the caption beneath this photograph.... if we went in for that kind of thing. The picture actually shows two Blackpool detectives examining the engine bay of a 1950s Ford Prefect. It is not known whether this was the latest addition to the police fleet, which seems likely, or whether the vehicle had been involved in some crime or other. Notice the optional spot lamps fitted to the car - particularly the passenger-side lamp which is thoughtfully adjusted to dazzle on-coming traffic! The roof of the vehicle has a rubberised fabric covering. Sometimes this indicates the presence of a sun-roof, but on cars built around the 1940s it is more often evidence of a technique used to cut down on the amount of steel used in vehicle construction.

Imperial Hotel - jewel in the crown of Blackpool's hotels

The Victorians built on a vast scale, a fact illustrated by three cast iron piers, a 518 feet tower and, not least, The Imperial, overlooking the sea on the north promenade.

It had its origins in a syndicate, the Blackpool Land & Building Company, which was formed in 1863 and bought land to create the Claremont Park Estate. Ambitious plans included the erection of the Imperial to stand in its own ground on the highest point of the land with a commanding position on the sea front. Shareholders agreed that the cost should not exceed £15,000.

By 1867, the hotel was let on a tenancy to Mr. William Beachy Head. The company advanced him £5,000 at five per cent interest for furnishings. The tariff then was three guineas a week and 4s 6d a day for servants.

There was a disappointing take up. The railway service was poor and other forms of transport negligible and the development of Blackpool as a seaside resort had only just begun.

The Land & Building Company persuaded the Lancashire and Yorkshire Railway Company to issue cheap weekend fares to Blackpool and things began to look up. In 1869, Charles Dickens spent a night at the Imperial during a tour of the north country giving readings from his works to packed audiences after a triumphant tour of the USA.

When Mr. Head relinquished his tenancy, the company failed to find another tenant. They appointed managers but still they had no success. Therefore, in 1872, a limited company was formed for a while. Maybe the lack of success of this latter venture had something to do with the conscientious objections of the majority of the shareholders to the granting of a liquor licence!

The hotel floundered financially until 1889 when, at last, shareholders received a dividend of 4%. Then, slowly, the Imperial began to flourish.

Improvements began. In 1901 Turkish and Russian baths and a sea water plunge bath were built in the basement and a ballroom was added which accommodated 400. Another wing of bedrooms was added three years later. Their comfort can be guessed at. For part of the First World War the Imperial was taken over by the government as an *officers'* hospital. After the war there was a wholesale renovation and, in 1925, more extensions. The government took over

Alexandra, whilst amongst statesmen to patronise the Imperial have been Churchill, Attlee, Macmillan, Douglas-Home, Wilson, Lady Thatcher, John Major and Tony Blair.

The hotel's Victorian grandeur remains. All renovation has been careful to blend traditional appearance with up-to-date facilities, which currently include 183 bedrooms, restaurants and bars, a fitness club with a heated swimming pool and fully equipped gymnasium. The Forte Venue Guarantee assures a superior range of business facilities.

The whole of Blackpool can take an enormous pride in the part the Imperial plays in the success of the town.

again during the second war, this time making the Imperial into officer accommodation.

When the directors regained possession eleven years later, costly improvements included the purchase of seven and a half miles of carpet. There has been constant renovation since. In 1958 the whole hotel was provided with central heating.

The quality of the accommodation can be judged by some of the guests. Royalty has visited, including the present Queen Mother and Princess

Above: The foyér as seen today. **Top left and bottom left:** *Two views of the sitting room, the top dating from the early part of the century and the bottom from today.* **Facing page, bottom left:** *An artist's impression of the hotel dating from the early 1900s.* **Facing page, top right:** *The foyér as seen at the turn of the century.*

British Aerospace - part of the town's aeronautical heritage

Warton Aerodrome, which plays a key role in the prestigious British Aerospace organisation is a mere 10 miles from Blackpool. In fact, it is rumoured that the top of Blackpool Tower can be seen from the road alongside.

Work first began on the Warton Aerodrome site around 1940. The airfield was required as a satellite for the RAF station at Squires Gate and was to consist of three runways and basic amenities. In 1941 the decision was taken to develop the Warton site into a Depot for the American Airforce and following the construction of longer runways and

Hangar facilities the site was handed over to the Americans in 1943

Base Air Depot 2, as Warton was known, had at its peak over 20,000 American servicemen based there, employed in a variety of technical trades. The principal function of the Depot was to prepare new aircraft prior to their delivery to front line units and also to undertake modification and repair work to existing aircraft. The types of aircraft handled ranged from small fighters to large, four-engined bombers.

The period 1943 to 1945 was a time of intense activity at Warton. At its peak the Depot was turning out aircraft quicker than the operating units could take them. At times, over 300 aircraft were parked outside along the perimeter tracks and both sides of the runways, with the smaller fighters often parked under the wings of the larger bombers to save space. Only the main runway was kept clear for take-offs and landings. A fleet

Above: A Douglas A20 Havoc seen flying over Blackpool during the Second World War. Left: Flying from Blackpool sands is an AVRO Bi-plane. Right: A wartime postcard, showing that Blackpool was as proud of its association with aircraft as it was of its more familiar landmarks.

Facing page, bottom right: American servicemen on parade in Talbot Square in 1943. Facing page, main picture: A group of American servicemen outside one of the hangars at Warton. Facing page, bottom left: The familiar face of Bing Crosby on a visit to Warton in 1944.

of 15,000 vehicles was used to transport people, parts and tools around the busy base.

As the war drew to a close a Technical Training School was established to enable servicemen to be retrained ready for their return to civilian life. At the same time, the aerodrome and its facilities was handed back to the RAF who established a Maintenance Unit there.

Nearby, in Preston, the English Electric Company was beginning to design the Canberra jet bomber. In order to support the development programme additional space was required and so the company leased some of the facilities at Warton in 1947 from the Air Ministry. It was from Warton on the 13th May 1949 that the Canberra Prototype first flew.

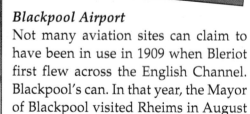

Blackpool Airport

Not many aviation sites can claim to have been in use in 1909 when Bleriot first flew across the English Channel. Blackpool's can. In that year, the Mayor of Blackpool visited Rheims in August for the Champagne Flying Week. His express intention was to arrange a similar event in Blackpool and by October 'Blackpool Aviation Week' was under way.

It had been jointly organised by the Blackpool Corporation and the Lancashire Aero Club and held on the site now occupied by Blackpool Airport

There were no established airports in Britain at that time and this was the first officially recognised air display to be held in the UK. Airman, Henry Farman, thrilled 200,000 spectators with a steady flight of 14 miles, seven

times round the airport. At the end of the week, he carried off the Grand Prize of Blackpool for a further flight of 24 laps (approximately 48 miles). This stood as the first official British record.

That first Aviation Week established Blackpool as a venue for aviation activities, since when there have been many changes both in operations and types of aircraft. From the early bi-planes and monoplanes of the aviation pioneers, it has been used by a variety of aircraft types including the Wellington Bomber and Hunter Jet Fighter, through to the present-day helicopters supplying the Morecambe Bay Gas Field.

A Flying Carnival was arranged in 1910, organised by the Lancashire Air Club. A week of competitions with daily prizes was organised, but because of adverse flying conditions the programme proved over-optimistic and it marked the end of Squires Gate as a centre for aviation for more than a decade.

The ground was used as a race course, with paddock, grandstand and clubhouse. The race course failed but the buildings were useful as a military convalescence home during the First World War. As many as 3,000 men were housed in huts built over the old race course. The area was handed back to the Clifton Estate in 1924.

The War had given aviation a great impetus and aircraft became firmly established in the public mind. This, combined with Blackpool's attraction for large crowds, led to pleasure flights being organised in the resort in 1919. They went from the South Shore under the auspices of A.V. Roe. Later the pleasure flights were transferred to Squires Gate and operated by the Lancashire School of Aviation.

At the Marton site, two years' hard work levelling and draining the land made it possible to build a clubhouse and hangar, which buildings survive today as part of Blackpool Zoo. The aerodrome occupied 120 acres at a cost to the Corporation of £39,000.

*Above: The Canberra was the first aeroplane manufactured at Warton after the Second World War. This one can be seen flying over Blackpool with the familiar sight of the Pleasure Beach beneath it. The Roller-Coaster has been sadly dwarfed in recent years by the likes of the Pepsi Max. **Facing page, main picture:** American Servicemen assembling engines at Warton during World War II. **Facing page, top right:** A promotional poster depicting thirty years at Squires Gate dating from the 1970s.*

Towlers - A 'moving' story!

A Preston man wandered into leafy Lytham in 1875, bought a landau, and set himself up in business. It blossomed into the biggest coach, taxi and haulage firm in the town. The man was Henry Towler.

His business flourished and soon he owned in the region of 30 horses. As well as being used for landau, they pulled two-wheeled carts for removals, sometimes to places as far away as Manchester. During these early days when he took people on to Marton Moss in his landau, his son, Thomas, became interested. Thomas had served his time as a joiner at

Myers-cough's and he built up the family business with coaches, lorries and carts.

Thomas was joined in the business by his wife Hannah 'Daisy' Davies from Woodplumpton, whom he married in 1920.

The next generation to take over was their son Harry and daughter Betty. Mrs. Johnson's first career was in accountancy, but, as a 17 year old, she drove a taxi before and after working at Latham's, sometimes finishing at four in the morning. It amused her husband, Crosby, that when she was out with him

she had to be in by midnight! Crosby remembered carting coal to Lytham Hospital and Westwood Miners' Home, Lytham mussels from the purification tanks on Lytham beach, staff to Moss Side, Lytham and St. Anne's Hospitals and schoolchildren who are now grandparents.

During the war, the firm worked for the government transporting munitions to various parts of Lancashire. It provided the mayoral car for 40 years.

The business continued to do well despite a fire that almost wiped it out in 1947. The largest fire in Lytham for ten years, it destroyed 13 vehicles including private and hire cars and two furniture vans. The horses were saved but the garage, wooden stables and hay loft in South Clifton Street were gutted. Sadly, the century-old family tradition was broken in 1984 when the last surviving Towler, Mrs. Betty Johnson sold out to Mr. and Mrs. Don Lunan. However, the original name was retained.

Following this change of ownership, the company continued for three years in the original premises. By this time, the removal and storage work had increased fourfold so new premises were taken on the outskirts of Lytham. Here, Towler's became the first removal firm to set up a local containerised storage facility, whilst the flourishing taxi side of the business was sold off.

In 1989, the company began a weekly removal service to and from Germany and, later, to other parts of Europe. In 1993 Towlers took over F. Sarti and Sons, two of its three owners having retired.

More space was needed for this acquisition so Towlers moved again to Wrea Green, still in the Fylde Borough. Since then work has extended to several government departments including the National Health Service.

In 1996, after acquiring B. Marshall Removals of Blackpool, the company's retiring owners, Don and Joyce Lunan, began disposing of the Towler Group to the Pantechnicon Group, a nationwide company specialising in corporate removals. Pantechnicon will keep the Towler name going and, uniquely, have given the latter an entirely separate legal identity within the group.

As their business expanded Towlers have taken great care not to forsake their many local customers. An example of customer loyalty was recently expressed by a lady who told her pensioner father that she was moving with Towlers. "I should think so!" the father replied. "They moved your grandparents in 1930 and we had no trouble then."

Facing page main picture: A delightful scene from the 1920s, showing one of the company's carts decorated for a local carnival.
Facing page small picture: Three employees from the 1970s.
Left: Returning from Rildalton Castle, Isle of Islay, Scottish home of Squire Clifton.

Chadwicks - helping to build Blackpool since the 1890s

Just over a century ago, in Chadwick's Row, St. Walburga's Road, Little Layton, James Chadwick ran his farm whilst his sons, Arthur and Daniel, began their joinery business. James had moved there in the 1880s from Burnley when he married.

His sons Daniel and Fred served apprenticeships as joiners for William Eaves and Arthur as a wheelwright in Staining.

Once qualified, Daniel and Arthur launched Chadwick Brothers in 1896, using the farms next to the family farmhouse as a sawmill and joiner's shop.

Its first commission was from a neighbour who wanted a new hinge on an old wooden box. This transaction marked the humble beginning of this well known Blackpool company.

Daniel's son Jim and Arthur's son William followed them into the business along with several other apprentices and the firm grew, becoming registered as a limited company in 1929.

During the 30s, Chadwick brothers had 400 employees and was responsible for building the Cliffs Hotel and the Red Lion Hotel at Bispham and the rebuilding of R.H.O. Hills on Bank Hey Street in Blackpool town centre.

The decline in building during the Second World War took the company away from the contracting business and the 1960s marked the start of the company's emphasis on retailing.

Above: Chadwick's timber store in Mowbray Drive, Blackpool. A recent advertisement stated rather proudly: We may be 100 years old but builders still fancy us!

Top left: Arthur Chadwick, who was a wheelwright in Staining before founding his own business in 1896.

Left: Chadwick's Row, St Walburga's Road, Little Layton. James Chadwick lived in the building on the left of the picture. His sons, Arthur and Daniel began the joinery business in the barn.

William's son Douglas was born in 1924. He qualified as a quantity surveyor and took the business from strength to strength.

His widow, Hilda, retains a keen interest and her son Andy was the one who took full advantage of the 1980s property boom and put Chadwick's firmly on the map in timber, DIY, decorating and reliable daily deliveries of everything from tacks to tiles, from wallpaper to wardrobes.

When he began work at the age of 14, the firm had been based on Mowbray Drive for almost a decade, taken there by his father.

Ironmongery has multiplied tenfold. The decor department stocks more than 4,000 paint colours. Kitchens can be designed, planned and purchased to the last door handle. Plastics, guttering, fascias, and uPVC cladding- were launched just three years ago. As Andy Chadwick says, 'We are part of Blackpool's history.'

*Left: Panelling can be cut to any size. **Top left:** Dougie Chadwick was the man credited with taking the post-war company to greater strengths throughout the 1950s, pulling it together and making the move to its present site from Chadwick's Row to Mowbray Drive. **Left:** Chadwick's have an extensive range of DIY and ironmongery products.*

Arnold School - 'Honour is the Reward Of Virtue'

A Prayer for the School- "...Grant that by the help of Thy Holy Spirit we may strive with one heart and mind to make this place more and more pleasing to Thee..." F. H. Sill.

This mixed, independent day school has ex pupils as diverse in their future careers as the English batsman, Tom Graveney, Sir William Lyons who founded Jaguar cars, Dr. Michael Smith who received the Nobel prize for Chemistry in 1993 and Chris Lowe, lead singer of The Pet Shop Boys. Its philosophy is evidently not to produce stereotypes.

The school was founded by Frank Truswell Pennington in 1896. Known initially as South Shore Collegiate School, it moved to its present site in Lytham Road when Pennington took over and gradually expanded the buildings of an earlier Victorian school. Pennington adopted the former school's name of Arnold House School after Dr. Thomas Arnold, Headmaster of Rugby School. The original Arnold House School had been set up by a Thomas Ward who had come to Blackpool from Leeds in 1868 and who was associated with the Wesleyan Methodist Movement. The name was later amended to Arnold School.

In 1903, William Henry Denham, the first boy on the school register in 1896, organised a football match between the school team and a team of old boys. Such was the spirit of the occasion that the Headmaster suggested the match be made an annual event. Twenty seven of the old boys met the following year to put the suggestion into a more permanent form. It was resolved that an Association of Arnold House Old Boys be formed.

By the time of his death in 1938, Pennington had given the school to the Old Boys who elected a Governing Council. From its inception, Arnold ha s attracted pupils of the highest calibre from the Fylde coast. In return, the school has given Lancashire many of its most distinguished citizens. Ernest Woodhouse-Smith, the son of the minister of a Unitarian church in Lytham was the first pupil to be awarded a university degree.

The Junior School was opened in 1920. The previous year, Frank Pennington had purchased a school in Horncliffe Road. On the first morning of term, 52 boys

School and the Sixth Form Centre. More recent developments have included the new Art and Music Departments, All-Weather Facilities, a state-of-the-art Design and Technology Centre and a Kindergarten Department for 3-year old boys and girls.

Arnold School's record of excellence has led to national and international recognition. With a record of one hundred years of outstanding educational achievement, Arnold School approaches the millennium with confidence as it combines the best of the new with the finest of the old. It never forgets its debt to its founder who embodied the school motto, 'Honor Virtutis Praemium'.

Facing page, top right: Frank Truswell Pennington, who founded the school in 1896. Facing page, bottom left: An early awards ceremony, dating from the end of the last century. Left: The school on Lytham Road. Below: A garden party, a regular feature of the early life of the school.

assembled. A separate preparatory form was also instituted and there was a kindergarten department in the mornings for children under seven. Mr Pennington presided at the first junior school speech day in 1923.

Successive headmasters have built on the solid foundations provided by F. T. Pennington. His immediate successor, Frank Holdgate, was to overcome the difficulties of war time Britain to establish his own reputation as well as pushing Arnold forward into a new age. Cameron Cochrane, headmaster 1973-9 took the decisive step towards co-education, a bold and decisive one.

Since being elected to membership of the Headmasters' Conference in 1945 the school has made a steady investment in new buildings. The post war years produced the School Memorial Hall, additional laboratories, a gymnasium, a new Junior

A century of service to Blackpool's meat trade

Neither the Cocker nor the Laycock families were originally born in the Blackpool area. John Cocker came from a long line of butchers of Darwen, near Blackburn.

He moved to Blackpool in the 1890s and opened a butcher's shop in Bolton Street, South Shore. He ran this for less than two years before moving to the newly built abattoir situated off Talbot Road.

The Laycocks from Barnsley used their own slaughterhouse behind Central Drive until 1908, when they too moved to Talbot Road.

In those days quite a lot of Blackpool's butchers slaughtered and prepared their own meat at the abattoir but gradually, as the two firms of Cocker and Laycock expanded, less of them used it.

In 1920, when John Cocker died, his sons, John and Harold continued the business, now trading as John Cocker Ltd. John's sons, Eric and John, joined them as they continued to serve the hundreds of local butchers. Cattle, sheep and pigs were bought from local farms and nearby auction marts.

Robin Winder, a Pilling farmer and cattle dealer was head buyer and served the company for over 50 years. After a while the company dealt in imported livestock, mostly from Ireland. The boat would deliver them to Fleetwood and the animals would be walked from there, via Bispham, up Knowle Hill to the abattoir.

With the introduction of controls imposed during the Second World War worked  under the ministry until restrictions were lifted in 1954. Then they combined, with shares equally distributed between the two families, and continued to operate from the old slaughter-house until its closure in the late sixties, when it no longer satisfied the Ministry's high standards.

During the early 1960s Eric and John's sister, Ellen joined the business for a short while. She was made head of the accounts department.

The FMC was started in 1954 by the National Farmers' Union as a farmers' co-operative for marketing livestock on a deadweight and grade basis.

high for them to afford. So, a friendly alliance of competitors was formed that went ahead with its own scheme. Cocker and Laycock Ltd got together with the Fatstock Marketing Corporation Ltd. to become the major shareholders of the new company.

Individual firms each used the abattoir facilities, paying the slaughtering fees to the new company.

The abattoir cost £150,000 and opened in April 1968. It had a modern production line for the slaughter of livestock and cleansing of carcasses according to the most recent Ministry of Health regulations. A staff of 20 had full toilet facilities and showers.

After the death of Mr. O.B. Laycock and the retirement of Mr. Edward Laycock in the early 70s, the Laycock family finally sold all their shares to R.P. Winder Ltd, another famous locally based meat wholesaling company.

The firm was now therefore trading as Cocker and Winder Ltd. The company continued to trade from the same premises, where a massive and costly project to upgrade the abattoir to EEC specifications was finally completed in 1992. Peter Winder and his partner Spencer Little made a large contribution to this huge refurbishment.

In 1993, after the death of John Cocker Snr, his sons John and Alan, with partners, Peter Winder and Spencer Little took over, buying out, their long-standing competitors FMC (Blackpool) in the following year. This meant a further name change to Cocker Blackpool Meat Company.

Facing page, top left: Founder of the company, John Cocker. Facing page, right: John Cocker, son of the founder and grandfather of the present director, Alan. Facing page, centre: Eric Cocker with his wife, Connie. Above left: Eric's brother, John and his wife (mother and father of Alan and John). Below: The modern fleet with the family (left to right) John with his son, John Paul and Alan Cocker.

Under this system, farmers could sell livestock to the FMC without going to auction and could get a fixed price for the carcass according to its weight and quality. The prices were worked out each week and published by the FMC. In 1962 the organisation became a public company and expanded by taking over Marsh & Baxter Ltd., a midland-based bacon curing, sausage and pie manufacturing firm which had already taken over C&P Harris (Colne) Ltd.

Plans were made to replace the old slaughterhouse but meat traders said that costs would be far too

Blackwood - solid as rock!

Apart from a brief period of casual work as a sugar boiler, Robert David Blackwood's early career had little to do with confectionery. As a teenager in Edinburgh, he enjoyed looking at the foreign ships in Leith Docks and when a German cargo ship bound for Australia needed a cabin boy he went off with it, going on from Australia to South Africa and later to work in Canada.

He was once awarded a medal for stopping a runaway horse galloping through the busy streets in Glasgow. Not your run-of-the-mill confectioner!

A labelling company employed him as a salesman in 1936. Then he moved on to selling essences, visiting many confectionery firms which, in 1944, brought him to Blackpool and Mr. Addy's 'rock' factory.

The factory was being run by women during the war. They did all the sugar boiling, lettering and 'rolling the lump'. They made smaller batches than the men had done so that they could cope with the weight.

The building comprised three floors, manufacturing on the ground floor, stock storage in the first floor and prize budgerigar breeding at the top! What would today's health inspectors make of that?

Since he had decided to sell his business, Mr. Addy did not require any essences. How much, Mr Blackwood demanded, did Mr Addy want for his business, and what was his sugar allocation? The latter question was important at the time because sugar was rationed and your quota governed how much you could produce. On being given the figures, Mr Blackwood decided to buy.

With the factory came a stall in Abingdon Street Market. Soon Mr Blackwood acquired another sweetshop. It was on Coronation Street and was owned by two old ladies who had no intention of selling. Impressed by the favourable position of the premises, just opposite the Winter Gardens, Mr Blackwood made the ladies a financial offer they could not refuse.

Far left: Robert David Blackwood, founder of Blackwood's rock company. *Left:* The sugar, glucose and water are poured into a large copper pan. In the old days this would have been heated by coke but now by steam. The mix is heated to a very high temperature, known as the 'crack' temperature because when a small piece is dropped in cold water it will snap or crack between the fingers. *Below:* White rock on a pulling machine. Used to aerate the rock, this process makes the rock go snowy white and opaque for use in the next process - lettering.

In 1952, he took in addition a rock stall on Blackpool Pleasure Beach, to demonstrate and sell. There was no machinery there and the rock was pulled by hand over a large hook at the front of the stall. An employee, 'Cobbie', made the crowds laugh, then, when the demonstration was finished, persuaded them to buy.

Over the years, various shops were rented for a season, then, in 1980, Blackwoods returned to Coronation Street, this time to larger premises. Business flourished, largely thanks to Bob Blackwood's original ideas, including cat face lollipops and names on Easter eggs long before Thornton's thought of it. At the height of 'Beatlemania' the company commissioned a packaging firm to print a quarter of a million bags with the faces of the Beatles. Round red clear lollies went inside them. Paul was sold out first!

By degrees, Bob Blackwood handed over the running of his business to his stepson, Geoffrey Race who is still managing director. He himself has been part of the rock industry for almost 40 years. At the tender age of 14 he was to be seen in the window of a shop demonstrating the art of chocolate dipping. Bob's son and namesake is a director of the business, working in the factory as production manager.

Mr Race led the business through the lull of the sixties and the expansion of the 70s and 80s, beginning a successful export trade to Australia and diversifying with a separate company, into the amusement business.

A director of both companies, Mrs Race plays an active role. Both management and employees pride themselves on supplying customers with a steady flow of good quality confectionery. They find the seasons seem to come and go quickly as Blackpool is an exciting place in which to do business.

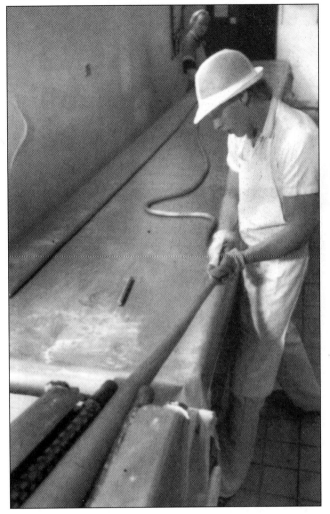

Above: The roll is expertly pulled out while in a revolving machine, the thickness varying depending on how thick the stick needs to be. The piece is then chopped to 30 foot lengths at which time it is passed to a specially designed cutter which measures the length at the same time as cutting. *Left:* Letters are formed and then placed together. The casing is rolled flat and the letters placed in the centre. Incidentally, the piece of rock shown would have weighed well over a hundredweight and needed two men to lift it into the batch roller.

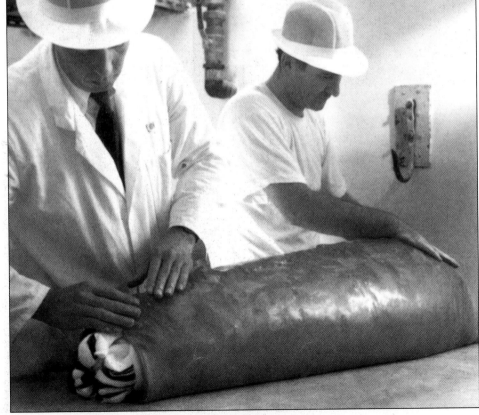

Lytham St Annes - home to the Football League

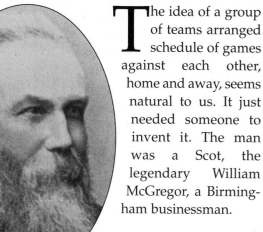

The idea of a group of teams arranged schedule of games against each other, home and away, seems natural to us. It just needed someone to invent it. The man was a Scot, the legendary William McGregor, a Birmingham businessman.

When he first formulated the idea of a national league, he omitted the word 'English' because he hoped that one day clubs from Scotland and Wales would also participate in the competition. Professionalism had spread through clubs in the north and midlands and it was apparent that clubs needed an assured income source if they were to be certain of being able to pay their players.

Before 1888, football had been a carefree affair. Even if two clubs had arranged a match there was no guarantee that they would both turn up, and when they did the game was often as much as an hour late in starting. The games lacked the regular competitive element that only a league system could bring.

Mr McGregor wrote to five leading clubs to suggest that stricter control was needed and recommended that a dozen of the more powerful clubs should form a league. The result was an informal meeting at Anderton's Hotel in Fleet Street, London. McGregor's proposal was accepted and the first formal meeting took place a month later, when the title 'The Football League' was adopted.

Of the clubs offering themselves for membership, twelve were accepted and three rejected. The first winners of the new competition were Preston North End and the idea of a league was an immediate success. In 1892, four more clubs were admitted to the original group and a second division of twelve clubs was formed.

By 1919-20 the first two divisions were brought up to 22 clubs in each. The third division appeared in 1920 and the fourth in 1958. After the resignation of the first division clubs to form their own Premier League in 1992 the remaining clubs were restructured

into first, second and third divisions which now contain 24 clubs each, 72 in all.

League headquarters

In the beginning the League was run from a terraced house in Hanley. Now it is run from a large red-brick building in its own grounds at Lytham St. Annes with a staff of 33. It is a democratic organisation with a powerful voice within the Football Association.

The staff in Lytham St. Annes deal with players' contracts, preparing the following season's fixtures (by computer these days), liaising with clubs to rearrange postponed games and making decisions about crowd safety and weather conditions.

The League appoints referees and their assessors, looks after its own complicated finances (levies, pension and life assurance funds, payment of revenue to clubs etc.) and deals with the press.

A vast filing system in the basement contains the minutes of every Management Committee meeting since 1888.

It is a democratic organisation. The Management Committee suggests policy but none of it becomes part of League regulations unless the clubs agree. Therefore, in one sense the history of the League is a chronicle of 111 years of disputes and dissension.

This is its strength rather than its weakness. Of course, all transactions are played out to a gallery of continual criticism and abuse from onlookers. It was ever thus. In 1888, a reporter called the League "Just a money-making circus".

Facing page, far left: William McGregor, founder of the Football League. *Facing page, main picture:* The board as seen in the 1960s. *Left:* A football crowd from the 1970s. One can feel the excitement which was clearly rising to fever pitch. *Below:* The headquarters in Lytham St. Annes, a charming looking, red-brick house.

Fifty years of service to the motorist

Peter joined him in 1970 after his student days and became Managing Director in 1984, the year the business moved to Ansdell Road and became the main Vauxhall dealer.

Not only do they sell the full range of new Vauxhall cars, light vans and recreational vehicles but they also offer Network Q vehicles at both locations. Network Q is a brand of used vehicles which prepares vehicles to the very highest standards backed up by a comprehensive warranty, 114 point check and a mileage verification certificate. Moorland also operate a department especially for the business user offering highly competitive deals and special finance terms as well as contract hire and leasing. They are also an accredited specialist for motability, providing vehicles for the disabled.

The Company's philosophy is to provide the very best in Aftersales service and as such operate a well

On the wall of the office that Peter Swire occupies as Managing Director of Moorland Motors hangs a simple water colour. It shows, set against a patch of green grass, the Swires Garage, started by Peter's father Bill Swire in 1947. It stood in Poulton New Road, quite a small concern, giving little hint of what was to come.

Today Bill Swire is still Chairman of Moorland Motors, Blackpool and their new facilities at Garstang Road East, Poulton. The company are now the main Vauxhall retailers for the Fylde Coast and as such have carried off a stream of awards. In 1995 they were awarded both Company of the

Year and Business of the Year at the Firm Partners' awards which were sponsored by First Leisure, the Evening Gazette and Radio Wave. They were the first Motor Retailer on the Fylde Coast to achieve ISO9002 and are Working towards achieving the Investors in People standard next year.

Still actively involved in the business, Bill first used the Moorland name in 1960 when he built the garage on Breck Road in Poulton.

repairs to the very highest standards. They operate from a purpose built unit on Poulton Industrial Estate with the very latest high tech equipment and trained staff and are authorised repairers to most leading insurance companies.

Customer Care is paramount to Moorland Motors. From the minute the customer purchases their vehicle, they commence onto the customer care programme, firstly experiencing a very detailed handover process and soon after are invited back to the dealership to an open evening. They can then take advantage of the privilege card scheme for their subsequent years of ownership.

At the firm's 35th anniversary, Peter Swire had this message for customers past, present and future. "We are very privileged to have the Vauxhall franchise for the Fylde Coast. I believe that the combination of the product we offer, coupled with the service of a caring locally owned family run business, provides the ideal combination. Our aim is to provide quality service at a competitive price. We realise that the service we give is the heart of the business, if we provide consistently high quality and exceed customer expectations, there's a good chance they'll come back for their next vehicle. Most of the business, fortunately, is repeat business. That speaks for itself".

run fully equipped workshop with factory trained staff. They offer fixed price servicing and repairs as well as MOT testing. This is backed up by a comprehensive stock of parts and accessories. A large fleet of courtesy vehicles keep their customers mobile during repairs.

Moorland are members of the Vauxhall Approved Accident Repair Centre programme and carry out accident damage

Facing page, small picture: From the early days of Swires Garage. *Facing page, main picture:* Another view of the same garage in the early 1950s. *Above left:* Poulton New Road in the early 1960s. *Left:* The garage in the late 1950s.

Banks Carrington - serving the resort's legal needs since 1879

Records show that in 1879 Mr. William Banks, a prominent Preston solicitor, had a branch office at 10, Church Street, Blackpool. By 1887 he had moved to 33, Church Street, and later, in 1892, to 45, Church Street.

From very small beginnings, the office prospered. Many important businessmen involved in Blackpool's evolution became clients. At the same time, while looking after the needs of these developers and entrepreneurs, the staff did not disregard the needs of the ordinary public of Blackpool, the landau drivers, the pleasure boat and bathing van attendants, the smallholders and the many hoteliers and boarding house operators.

The founder of the firm, William Banks, died in 1893 and, by 1896, the firm of W. Banks & Company, now looked after by Mr. Edward Charles Banks and Mr. John Underhill, had moved to 16, Birley Street. Shortly afterwards, Mr. Harry Cartmell, a former assistant of William Banks, took over the running of the Blackpool office. Since that time, the Cartmell

family through three generations have continued to look after the legal needs of the Blackpool and Fylde coast population. Harry Cartmell, later to become Sir Harry, shared his time between the Blackpool and Preston offices combining these activities with the duties of being Mayor of Preston between 1914 and 1917.

In 1931, the firm of W. Banks & Company finally moved to its present premises where it has remained. These premises, built in 1869, were intended for guesthouse accommodation. Along with most others along Edward Street they were converted into professional offices.

Lately the firm has changed its name, following the official separation of the Blackpool and Preston offices. Under its new title, Banks Carrington & Co., it is still catering for the needs of the developed and developing businesses of Blackpool as well as the needs of the ordinary population.

The firm prides itself on providing a friendly and efficient service, offering home visits or out of hours appointments where necessary and being at all times approachable by all strata of Blackpool and Fylde society.

Far left: Mr Harry Cartmell in an official pose during his mayoral reign.

Left: This certificate was awarded to Mr Harry Cartmell when he was elected Mayor of Preston. He remained in this position for three years between 1914 and 1917.

Forty years of service to local individuals

Although this business was incorporated in 1957, it is possible to trace its roots back to the 1920s when the founder, James Ingham Badger began his career in Manchester with an insurance broking house, Donald Moore's & Company Ltd.

Jim Badger had become managing director when this firm was acquired by a large national broker. Not wishing to be part of this amalgamation, he set up Ingham Badger Ltd. in an office in St. Anne's on Sea. The firm is proud to be dealing with some of the same companies who patronised him in the 1920s.

Established in its present form in 1957, the business offers independent and impartial advice. It is conveniently situated in town-centre offices in Caunce Street which are

equipped with the latest computerised systems, giving direct, on-line access to insurers. A full range of general insurance needs is offered.

When Ingham Badger Ltd. first launched its Tower Hoteliers Policy, it created a new deal designed to meet the specific needs of the holiday industry in Blackpool and the Fylde. The policy is unique to Ingham Badger Ltd. and provides excellent cover at very competitive premiums. It has operated

successfully since 1988. One of its important selling points is its team of local builders, plumbers, glaziers and so on. They will carry out all repairs quickly so that the least possible business is lost whilst the disaster, whatever it might be is dealt with.

Above: The company's premises in Caunce Street.
Left: The attractive reception area gives the customer a feeling of confidence in the company.

Lancashire County Council
Blackpool Reference Library

Blackpool Reference Library houses a wealth of reference sources including encylopaedias, directories etc., along with a business information service. A particular feature of the library is its vast collection of information relating to Blackpool and the surrounding areas. Included are maps, photographs, newspaper runs and census records. Enquiries on any aspect of local history are always welcome.

Opening Hours are as follows:
Monday: *10.00am to 5.00pm*
Tuesday: *10.00am to 7.00pm*
Wednesday: *10.00am to 5.00pm*
Thursday: *10.00am to 7.00pm*
Friday: *10.00am to 5.00pm*
Saturday: *10.00am to 5.00pm*

Car parking in the immediate vicinity of the library comprises mostly on-street parking with a one-hour limit during office hours. A small pay and display car park is located next door to the library and Art Gallery on Queen Street.

Queen Street, Blackpool FY1 1PX
Telephone: 01253 23977 Fax: 01253 751670